Political Prisoners

Series Titles

- **The History of Punishment and Imprisonment**
- **Juveniles Growing Up in Prison**
- **Political Prisoners**
- **Prison Alternatives and Rehabilitation**
- **Prison Conditions Around the World**
- **The Treatment of Prisoners and Prison Conditions**
- **The True Cost of Prisons**
- **Unequal Justice**
- **Women Incarcerated**

Political Prisoners

FOREWORD BY **Larry E. Sullivan, PhD**

Associate Dean, John Jay College of Criminal Justics

BY **Roger Smith**

MASON CREST

Mason Crest
450 Parkway Drive, Suite D
Broomall, PA 19008
www.masoncrest.com

Printed and bound in the United States of America.

First printing
9 8 7 6 5 4 3 2 1

Series ISBN: 978-1-4222-3781-6
Hardcover ISBN: 978-1-4222-3784-7
ebook ISBN: 978-1-4222-7999-1

Library of Congress Cataloging-in-Publication Data

Names: Smith, Roger, 1959 August 15- author.
Title: Political prisoners / by Roger Smith ; foreword by Larry E. Sullivan, PhD, Associate Dean, John Jay College of Criminal Justics.
Description: Broomall, PA : Mason Crest, [2018] | Series: The prison system | Includes index.
Identifiers: LCCN 2016054101| ISBN 9781422237847 (hardback) | ISBN 9781422237816 (series) | ISBN 9781422279991 (ebook)
Subjects: LCSH: Political prisoners--Juvenile literature.
Classification: LCC HV8665 .S63 2018 | DDC 365/.45--dc23

Developed and Produced by Print Matters Productions, Inc.
(www.printmattersinc.com)

Cover and Interior Design: Tom Carling, Carling Design
Additional Text: Briane Boone

Contents

KEY ICONS TO LOOK FOR:

Words to understand: These words with their easy-to-understand definitions will increase the reader's understanding of the text while building vocabulary skills.

Sidebars: This boxed material within the main text allows readers to build knowledge, gain insights, explore possibilities, and broaden their perspectives by weaving together additional information to provide realistic and holistic perspectives.

Educational Videos: Readers can view videos by scanning our QR codes, providing them with additional educational content to supplement the text. Examples include news coverage, moments in history, speeches, iconic sports moments and much more!

Text-dependent questions: These questions send the reader back to the text for more careful attention to the evidence presented there.

Research projects: Readers are pointed toward areas of further inquiry connected to each chapter. Suggestions are provided for projects that encourage deeper research and analysis.

Series glossary of key terms: This back-of-the book glossary contains terminology used throughout this series. Words found here increase the reader's ability to read and comprehend higher-level books and articles in this field.

Foreword

Prisons have a long history, one that began with the idea of evil, guilt, and atonement. In fact, the motto of one of the first prison reform organizations was "Sin no more." Placing offenders in prison was, for most of the history of prison systems, a ritual for redemption through incarceration; hence the language of punishment takes on a very religious cast. The word *penitentiary* itself comes from the concept of penance, or self-punishment to make up for a past wrong. When we discuss prisons, we are dealing not only with the law, but with very strong emotions and reactions to acts that range from minor crimes, or misdemeanors, to major crimes, or felonies, such as murder and rape.

Prisons also reflect the level of the civilizing process through which a culture travels, and it tells us much about how we treat our fellow human beings. The 19th-century Russian author Fyodor Dostoyevsky, who was a political prisoner, remarked, "The degree of civilization in a society can be measured by observing its prisoners." Similarly, Winston Churchill, the British prime minister during World War II, said that the "treatment of crime and criminals is one of the most unfailing tests of civilization of any country."

For much of the history of the American prison, we tried to rehabilitate or modify the criminal behavior of offenders through a variety of treatment programs. In the last quarter of the 20th century, politicians and citizens alike realized that this attempt had failed, and they began passing stricter laws, imprisoning people for longer terms, and building more prisons. This movement has taken a great toll on society. Beginning in the 1970s federal and state governments passed mandatory minimum sentencing laws, stricter habitual offender legislation, and other "tough on crime" laws that have led today to the incarceration in prisons and jails of approximately 2.3 million people, or an imprisonment rate of 720 per 100,000 people, the highest recorded level in the world. This has led to the overcrowding of prisons, worse living conditions, fewer educational programs, and severe budgetary problems. Imprisonment carries a significant social cost since it splits families and contributes to a cycle of crime, violence, drug addiction, and poverty. The Federal Sentencing Reform Act of 1984 created a grid of offenses and crime categories for sentencing that disallowed mitigating circumstances. This grid was meant to prevent disparate sentences for similar crimes. The government made these guidelines mandatory, thereby taking most discretionary sentencing out of the hands of judges who previously could give a wider range of sentences, such as one year to life, and allow for some type of rehabilitation. The unintended consequences of this legislative reform in sentencing was the doubling of the number of incarcerated people in the United States. Combined with the harsh sentences on drug offenders, almost half of the prisoners in the federal system are narcotics offenders, both violent and nonviolent, traffickers and users. States followed suit in enacting the harsh guidelines of the federal government in sentencing patterns. "Life without parole" laws and the changes in parole and probation practices led to even more offenders behind bars. Following the increase in the number of incarcerated offenders, more and more prisons were built with the aid of federal funds and filled to the brim with both violent and nonviolent offenders. In addition,

many states handed over penal custody to the new private for-profit prisons that stemmed from mass incarceration.

In the 21st century officials, politicians, and the public began to realize that such drastic laws wrought much harm to society. With the spread of long-term imprisonment, those who had spent decades in prison were unemployable after release. Their criminal histories followed them and made it difficult if not impossible to find gainful employment. Therefore, they entered the criminal world continually and thus sped up the vicious cycle of crime-imprisonment-release-crime-punishment. America was reaching the tipping point; something had to give.

In response to this growing trend of harsh sentencing, for example, the Supreme Court led the way between 2005 and 2016 with decisions banning the death penalty for juveniles (Roper v. Simmons, U.S. 551 [2005]), life sentence without parole for juveniles not convicted of homicide (Graham v. Florida, 130 S. Ct. 2011 [2010]); and life without parole for juveniles (Miller v. Alabama and Jackson v. Hobbes 132 S. Ct. 2455 [2012] and Montgomery v. Louisiana 135 S.Ct. 1729 [2015]). Behavioral psychologists and other officials do not consider juveniles capable of making fully formed decisions, and the Supreme Court has recognized the developmental differences that excuses full individual responsibility and applies to their actions the philosophic principle of just deserts. Many states (90 percent of prisoners are under state, not federal jurisdiction) are beginning to take action by reducing harsh mandatory sentences for adults. Most states, for example, have gone toward the decriminalization or legalization of marijuana, with lighter penalties for possession of the drug. Since most prisoners in state institutions are violent, however, contemporary America is caught in a dilemma with which many academics and governmental policy makers are aggressively grappling.

All these are reasons why this series on the prison system is extremely important for understanding the history and culture of the United States. Readers will learn all facets of punishment: its history; the attempts to rehabilitate offenders; the increasing number of women and juveniles in prison; the inequality of sentencing among the races; attempts to find alternatives to incarceration; the high cost, both economically and morally, of imprisonment; and other equally important issues. These books teach us the importance of understanding that the prison system affects more people in the United States than any institution, other than our schools.

LARRY E. SULLIVAN, PHD
Associate Dean
Chief Librarian
John Jay College of Criminal Justice
Professor of Criminal Justice
Graduate School and University Center
City University of New York

☑ Political Imprisonment

As defined in *The Oxford History of the Prison*, a political prisoner is "someone who is incarcerated for his or her beliefs." Because political prisoners' ideas challenge or pose a threat, either real or perceived, to the state, they are imprisoned or held under **house arrest**. The experiences of real political prisoners recounted in this book give a sense of the terrible situations these men and women are forced to endure.

> *Now I swing between the deepest resentment and the sincere wish to feel no more hatred. Hatred eats you up. . . . Hatred will never enable me to make up for the lost years.*
>
> —MALIKA OUFKIR

Malika Oufkir has experienced things few people could even imagine. For a few years, she lived a fairy tale, and then for two decades, her life was a nightmare. She,

After spending years locked away as a political prisoner with her family, Malika Oufkir is finally free.

her five siblings, and her mother were political prisoners held under unbearable conditions as punishment for her father's crime.

Malika, whose name means "Princess" in Arabic, was born in 1953 in Morocco. Her mother loved movies, shopping, horseback riding, and Elvis Presley; her father, Muhamed Oufkir, held many important government positions and was close to the king. When Malika was five years old, King Mohammed V saw her playing with his daughter. The king told Malika's parents, "I wish to adopt your daughter"; he wanted her to be a playmate for his child. Immediately, she moved into the palace. She had the best of everything—education, toys, and royal treatment—yet she could not leave the palace.

When she was 16, Malika rebelled against the limitations of living in the royal court, and the king allowed her to leave the palace. For the next few years, she lived a dream, as her parents were wealthy and famous, and she was young and beautiful. She traveled to Paris and the United States, where famous politicians and movie stars paid attention to her. She dreamed of making movies in Hollywood, and she might have done so if cruel fate had not intervened.

On August 16, 1972, Malika was relaxing with friends in her house in Casablanca when she switched on the television; in a single moment, her life changed forever. The news announcer said an unsuccessful **coup** had taken place against the king, Hasssan II, led by Malika's father, who had become a senior military officer and minister of defense. Shortly after, her father called Malika, telling her that he was proud of her and loved her. The next day, Malika was staring at her father's bullet-ridden body, and almost at once, the king took her, her siblings, and her mother into custody.

On Christmas Eve of that year, a big car with blacked-out windows, escorted by armed police, drove the Oufkir family to a secret desert prison. Malika writes: "This was a country where they locked up young children for their father's crimes. We were entering the world of insanity." At age 19, Malika was the oldest child; her youngest brother, Abdellatif, was only 3 years old. They had become the "disappeared."

Years in Prisons

From 1973 to 1977 the Moroccan government imprisoned the Oufkirs in a ruined fortress in Tamattaght. The summer heat was stifling and the winter cold biting. Huge rats crawled into the prison, where the mother and children beat them off with sticks. "I thought there were limits to human suffering," Malika Oufkir writes, but at their next place of imprisonment, "I was to discover there were none."

For 10 years, King Hassan II held the Oufkirs at Bir-Jdid Prison, near Casablanca, each in solitary confinement. The children had smuggled pigeons from Tamattaght to Bir-Jdid, as these pets helped them to feel less lonely. The guards at Bir-Jdid discovered the pigeons and made a cruel game of killing them in front of the children. Little Abdellatif, who had just turned eight, tried unsuccessfully to kill himself.

The family lived in wretched conditions: wounds, illnesses, improper sanitation, lack of privacy, cockroaches, mosquitoes, mice, and rats plagued them. On top of that, the guards practically starved them to death. "Hunger humiliates, hunger debases," Malika writes. "Hunger turns you into a monster. We were always hungry."

For almost a decade, the mother and children fought against insanity. Malika made up stories they passed secretly from cell to cell as a way of remembering their humanity and relieving the maddening boredom of solitary confinement. Finally, they were all at their wits' end. The mother and oldest brother attempted suicide, but they were too weak to succeed. At that point, the Oufkirs decided their only hope of survival was escape.

Using a spoon, a knife handle, the lid of a sardine tin, and an iron bar from one of the beds, they began to tunnel between their cells and under the walls of their prison. Each morning, they carefully replaced the stones atop their tunnel so guards would not notice. On April 19, 1987, Malika and three of her siblings shoved their bodies through the narrow tunnel, under the walls, and up into the dark desert night—they were free.

Escape to a Strange Kind of Freedom

Although they had escaped, the four Oufkir siblings had to endure almost a week of terrifying, frustrating efforts to make contact with people who could help them reach **asylum**. They attempted to contact family members, former friends, and foreign embassies, but their efforts to find refuge failed repeatedly; when they most desperately needed help, it seemed no one would assist them.

The Oufkirs' salvation came about due to an official visit to Morocco by the French president, François Mitterrand. The four siblings contacted a member of the president's party, and President Mitterrand sent them a message: "You should be very proud of yourselves because while there are millions of children who are persecuted, massacred, and imprisoned in the world, you will be remembered as the only ones who did not give up and continued to fight to the end."

France publicized the Oufkirs' plight, and though the Moroccan police soon found them, King Hassan II did not dare send them back to prison while the world was watching. He released their mother and the other two siblings, and they all lived for the next five years in what Malika calls "a strange kind of freedom," officially free to go anywhere in Morocco yet continually followed by police, their phones tapped, their friends interrogated, and every step of their lives under surveillance. Finally, several of the Oufkir children managed to marry citizens of other countries and obtain legal emigration for the other family members out of Morocco. They were genuinely free at last, but the scars of decades in prison would continue to haunt them.

Malika is now married to a Frenchman and lives in Miami with their two children. According to a recent U.S. Department of State Report on Human Rights Practices, in Morocco, "Although progress continued in some areas, the human rights record remained poor in other areas. . . . The Constitution does not prohibit arbitrary arrest or detention, and police continued to use these practices."

After her release, Malika Oufkir felt obligated to educate the world about her family history and imprisonment. Since her liberation, she has written two books, Stolen Lives: Twenty Years in a Desert Jail, *which tells about her incarceration, and* Freedom: The Story of My Second Life, *which describes her life after incarceration.*

Famous Political Prisoners in History

The term *political prisoner* is sometimes confused with another expression, *prisoner of conscience*, but they are not the same thing. A political prisoner is someone jailed primarily because of his or her beliefs, but a political prisoner could also have engaged in violent acts. Contrasting with this, a prisoner of conscience is jailed because of his or her beliefs but has not engaged in any form of violence.

To illustrate the difference, let's look at Nelson Mandela, who became one of history's most famous political prisoners when the South African government incarcerated him for 27 years for opposing the practice of **apartheid**. Amnesty International (amnesty.org) refused to categorize Mandela as a prisoner of conscience because some of his fellow activists in organizations that he belonged to advocated violence in their struggle for racial justice. Dr. Martin Luther King Jr., on the other hand, who steadfastly opposed violence in his fight for racial equality in the United States, was considered both a political prisoner and a prisoner of conscience when held in the Birmingham, AL, jail in 1963.

Other famous political prisoners include the American writer and antiwar activist Henry David Thoreau, who was jailed for two nights in July 1846 for failure to pay taxes that would go to fund the Mexican-American War, and the Quaker leader William Penn, who was jailed in England in the 1660s for his religious beliefs. Penn went on to found the colony of Pennsylvania, whose charter, drafted by Penn, among other things guaranteed freedom of religion and freedom from unjust imprisonment.

Whether someone is a "political prisoner" depends on one's perspective. In the 21st century, most national governments agree that political imprisonment is immoral; likewise, most governments deny holding political prisoners.

Henry David Thoreau—poet, abolitionist, historian, and tax resister.

William Penn—philosopher, Quaker, and founder of Pennsylvania.

The Century of Political Imprisonment: the 1900s

During World War I and the decade that followed, the United States had a number of political prisoners, those labeled "radicals" and opposed to the war. Eugene Debs was a famous political prisoner of that time. While in prison in 1920, he received almost a million votes as the presidential nominee of the Socialist Party.

In June 1918 Debs gave a speech in Canton, OH, protesting against the war. In it he also spoke about the right of free speech guaranteed in the Bill of Rights in questioning the policies and actions of the government:

> *To speak for labor; to plead the cause of the men and women and children who toil; to serve the working class, has always been to me a high privilege; a duty of love. ...I realize that, in speaking to you this afternoon, there are certain limitations placed upon the right of free speech. I must be exceedingly careful, prudent, as to what I say, and even more careful and prudent as to how I say it. I may not be able to say all I think; but I am not going to say anything that I do not think. I would rather a thousand times be a free soul in jail than to be a sycophant and coward in the streets.*

Following this speech, Debs was arrested under the Espionage Act of 1917 and accused of trying to prevent the drafting of soldiers into the army. He was convicted and

American Political Prisoner Eugene Debs

Learn about the man who ran for president from prison.

sentenced to 10 years in prison. His defense argued that Debs's antiwar speech was protected by the Bill of Rights and that the Espionage Act, which made such talk illegal, was unconstitutional. His case went to the U.S. Supreme Court. In ruling in favor of the government, Justice Oliver Wendell Holmes stated: "When a nation is at war, many things that might be said in times of peace . . . will not be endured so long as men fight and no court could regard them as protected by any constitutional right." In other words, the circumstances of war might override the ordinary constitutional rights of U.S. citizens. This principle is significant as it affects the likelihood of political imprisonment during war, and it is still controversial today.

In 1917 the Russian tsar was overthrown, and in October of that year the Bolsheviks, or Communists, seized power. In the United States, national officials responded to the "Red Scare" by imprisoning Communist Party members and other activists. In 1919 and 1920 the U.S. government arrested more than 3,000 people for their communist or other "radical" tendencies.

Eugene Debs—labor organizer and socialist leader.

The Gulag

At the same time, the Bolsheviks in Russia were imprisoning or executing peasants, soldiers, and politicians, finishing off the opposition to their recent revolution. In 1928 Joseph Stalin took over leadership of the Russian Communist Party and increased the scope of political persecution and imprisonment. By 1938 the Russian government had incarcerated an estimated seven million people, or 1 of every 15 Russian citizens.

Stalin's massive political imprisonment was about to be overshadowed by even greater horrors in Germany. What became known as the Holocaust was the attempt by Adolf Hitler and the Nazi Party in Germany, before and during World War II, to exterminate all persons deemed "undesirable" by the party. No one is sure of the exact numbers, but historians estimate that the Nazis killed between 10 million and fourteen million people, mostly Jews. The death camps were the primary tools for this slaughter; these were facilities imprisoning men, women, and children for the purposes of slave labor or death in gas chambers. The death camps were also factories, where Nazis processed the corpses of their victims to create products for the war effort. In the entirety of human history, the Holocaust ranks as one of the very worst atrocities.

After the war, Russia continued to send men, women, and children to the Gulag, a network of forced labor camps in Siberia used mostly for political prisoners who opposed the Soviet state. More than a million people died in these camps, where the government forced them to do harsh labor logging or mining and kept them underfed and poorly sheltered. Eighty percent of prisoners died during their first months in the Gulag.

Political historians call the closing years of the 20th century "the human rights era." After the war, trials of the Nazi death camp guards alerted the world to the importance of rights for political prisoners. In 1948 the United Nations adopted the Universal Declaration of Human Rights. Only three countries—the Soviet Union, South Africa, and Saudi Arabia—failed to support the declaration. By the end of the 20th century, apartheid had ended in South Africa, along with the massive incarceration of political opponents to that system of segregation. Communism collapsed in Eastern Europe, ending mass incarceration of political prisoners in the former Soviet Union.

Not a Thing of the Past

Well into a new millennium, political imprisonment is far from over. According to the 2016 Freedom House (freedomehouse.org) report "Freedom in the World," Cuba, Libya, North Korea, Saudi Arabia, Sudan, Syria, and Turkmenistan are among the nations most notorious for political imprisonment. These are by no means the only offenders. According to the report, "The world in 2015 was battered by overlapping crises that contributed to the tenth consecutive year of decline in global freedom." In the following chapters, we meet some of the important people who have served time as political prisoners in history, as well as some of the brave women and men who continue to suffer imprisonment for their beliefs.

Text-Dependent Questions

1. Who ran for president as a Socialist candidate for president of the United States while in prison for antiwar activities?
2. What percentage of Russian citizens were incarcerated under the rule of Joseph Stalin?
3. How many people are estimated to have been killed by the Nazi regime in the Holocaust?

Research Projects

1. Investigate another example in history of mass incarcerations or persecutions like the Holocaust.
2. Research some of the countries today that are most associated with incarcerating political prisoners? What do they have in common?

2 Political Prisoners Who Shaped World History

We do not usually think of prisoners as moral leaders. However, political prisoners are often people of extraordinary moral strength; they choose to speak out for their beliefs rather than enjoy the comforts of freedom. For this reason, some of the outstanding political and social leaders of the 20th and 21st centuries were political prisoners for a time. These are their stories.

Taking a Stand for Freedom: Mohandas Gandhi

Mohandas Gandhi was born on October 2, 1869, the youngest of six children, in a small town near Bombay, India. The world knows him today as Mahatma Gandhi:

In 1893 Mohandas Gandhi traveled to South Africa to work as a lawyer for Muslim Indian traders. This photo was taken in 1900, 15 years before Gandhi returned to India.

Mahatma is an honorary Hindu title that means "holy" or "wise" and should not be confused with his first name.

As a young man, he was timid and struggled with his grades, but he managed to be the first child in his family to finish high school. After graduation, a friend told Gandhi he should go to England and earn a law degree there. His brother sold land and Gandhi's wife sold her jewelry to pay for his trip to England.

After attaining his degree in law in England, Gandhi went to South Africa to work on his first law case. In that country, something happened that changed the entire direction of Gandhi's life. South Africa at the time practiced apartheid, a system of racial discrimination similar to that in the southern United States at that time. Gandhi purchased a first-class ticket for the train trip from Durban to Johannesburg. When a train worker came to look at his ticket, he ordered Gandhi to leave first class and move to a poorer car, because the government did not allow "coloreds," including people of Indian descent, to travel first class. Gandhi refused to move: he had paid for first class, and he insisted on staying there. The train personnel kicked him off the train in the middle of a cold winter night.

Until this incident, Gandhi had shown little interest in politics, but feeling the sting of discrimination, he committed himself to the fight for racial and gender equality. He spent the next 22 years opposing discrimination in South Africa. He worked for a newspaper and wrote countless articles that showed how Indians and other people of color were mistreated.

By 1915 Gandhi was well known for his writing on behalf of justice in South Africa. His native country, India, was a British colony, and many Indians felt Britain was using India selfishly, not for the benefit of Indians. Influential Indians persuaded Gandhi to return to his homeland and work for the freedom of his people.

When a Jail Is a Temple

From May 1930 to May 1933, the British government imprisoned Gandhi and several of his fellow activists at Yeravda Prison. Louis Fischer, in his biography *Gandhi: His Life and Message for the World*, wrote:

> The Mahatma always obeyed the prison rules strictly as well as his own rule not to agitate from prison. Since he could not be a politician, he concentrated on being the saint. . . . After a while, Gandhi began to write down his thoughts on God and the ideal conduct of man: these were later published in a book called *Yeravda Mandir*. Mandir *means temple. A jail where God is discussed and worshiped becomes a temple.*

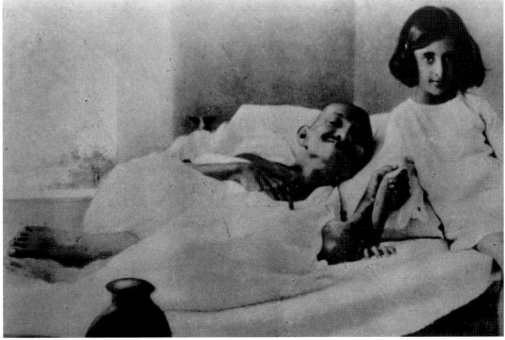

Gandhi and Indira Gandhi, the daughter of India's first prime minister, Jawarhalal Nehru, during his fast of 1924. Indira Gandhi also later served as prime minister.

Before leaving South Africa, Gandhi had become convinced that ruling governments do not give up power or treat poor people fairly unless people confront them directly. At the same time, he was committed to peace: Gandhi did not believe that mistreated people could achieve anything good through violence. He developed a practice called Satyagraha, which means "insistence on truth using nonviolent methods." Satyagraha might involve such methods as strikes, **boycotts,** and peaceful demonstrations. After returning to India, Gandhi began to call on his fellow citizens to use such means to convince Britain to free India. At the same time, he opposed practices common to Hindus. Most Hindus believed in the **caste** system, a form of religious-based discrimination against poor people, and many Hindus practiced discrimination against women as well. Gandhi was committed to a society where there would be no discrimination due to race, caste, religion, or gender—all persons would receive equal treatment.

Gandhi's campaign for liberty and equal rights landed him repeatedly in prison. Shall Gandhi Sinha, an expert on Gandhi, writes:

> *Gandhi himself was jailed many times, adding up to a total of 7 years during his lifetime, but he did not mind it. He used that period for rest*

and reflection. He kept writing for his papers. . . . Sometimes he was prevented from writing for his papers, but the government discovered that this created tremendous agitation in the public. The government found Gandhi to be a greater threat while he was imprisoned.

While in Yeravda Prison, Gandhi undertook one of his most important and dramatic political actions. On September 20, 1932, he determined to fast until he died or the British chose to end the practice of separate elections for untouchables (members of India's lowest caste). He believed that separate elections for different castes continued the practice of class discrimination. After six days, as Gandhi was nearing death, the British rulers agreed to end separate elections.

In 1947 India gained independence, ending 200 years of British domination. It was a major victory for Gandhi and his practices of nonviolent social change. A year later a fellow Hindu assassinated the Mahatma, angered by Gandhi's insistence on equality between castes. Gandhi, a political prisoner for seven years, had won freedom for all his fellow citizens and set an example of nonviolent change that others, including Dr. Martin Luther King Jr., would follow.

The Dream Lives On: Dr. Martin Luther King Jr.

In 1959 a young Baptist minister, Martin Luther King Jr., traveled to India and spoke with Prime Minister Jawaharlal Nehru and other people who had been associates of Mahatma Gandhi. The visit convinced King that Gandhi's philosophy of nonviolence was the only approach appropriate for African Americans in their fight to gain **civil rights**.

Martin Luther King Jr. after meeting with President Lyndon Johnson at the White House to discuss civil rights, 1963.

Civil Disobedience

One may ask: "How can you advocate breaking some laws and obeying others?" The answer lies in the fact that there are two types of laws: just and unjust. I would be the first to advocate obeying just laws. One has not only a legal but a moral responsibility to obey just laws. Conversely, one has a moral responsibility to disobey unjust laws. I would agree with St. Augustine that "an unjust law is no law at all."

–DR. MARTIN LUTHER KING JR.,
"LETTER FROM BIRMINGHAM JAIL"

The following year, police in Atlanta, GA, arrested King with a group of young people protesting **segregation** at a department store lunch counter. Although the city dropped charges, a court sentenced King to serve time at Reidsville State Prison Farm on the excuse that he had violated his probation for a minor traffic ticket issued several months earlier. People around the country expressed their concern and anger at this jailing and blamed President Dwight Eisenhower for failing to intervene. John F. Kennedy, the Democratic presidential nominee, used his influence to get Dr. King released.

In Birmingham, AL, in the spring of 1963, Dr. King and his followers continued their campaign to end segregation. Their protests gained sympathy around the nation when news reports showed police turning dogs and fire hoses on the unarmed demonstrators. The police jailed Dr. King along with large numbers of his supporters. While imprisoned, Dr. King wrote one of his best-known works, "Letter from Birmingham Jail," which explained the methods used by the civil rights movement, especially nonviolent resistance. King's tireless work to keep civil rights in the public discussion (along with leading many protests, including the March on Washington in 1963 and the Memphis Sanitation Workers Strike of 1968) led to many sweeping reforms in federal law that aimed to eliminate racism at the government level, including the Civil Rights Act of 1964, the Voting Rights Act of 1965, and the Fair Housing Act of 1968. Tragically, King was assassinated at a Memphis hotel in April 1968.In honor of his devotion to civil rights, in 1983 Congress made the third Monday in January (near the period of King's January 15th birthday) a federal holiday.

From his cell in the Birmingham Jail, Martin Luther King Jr. spent much of his time reflecting and writing about the methods used by the civil rights movement. Today he is recognized as the father of the movement—still an ongoing fight to this day.

South Africa United: Nelson Mandela

Nelson Mandela, the late president of South Africa and a Nobel Peace Prize winner, said his greatest pleasure was watching the sun set while listening to classical music. Why did he take such pleasure in ordinary moments? For 27 years, Mandela was a political prisoner, locked alone during daytime hours and denied the pleasures of music.

Nelson Rolihlahla Mandela was born in a village in Umtata, South Africa, on July 18, 1918. He went to school, earned his law degree, and as a young man joined the African National Congress (ANC), an organization dedicated to ending the unjust system of apartheid that controlled every aspect of South African life. Apartheid, or "separation," forced the majority of South Africans—native people of color—to live in inferior homes, attend inferior schools, and receive inferior medical care compared to their white minority fellow citizens, who ran the government and army.

A New Life

As I walked through those gates I felt—even at the age of seventy-one—that my life was beginning anew. My ten thousand days of imprisonment were at last over.

—NELSON MANDELA, DESCRIBING THE DAY OF
HIS RELEASE FROM PRISON

Influenced by Gandhi's success in freeing India by nonviolent means, the ANC at first attempted to follow the Indian leader's peaceful methods in their struggle for equality. However, the white government responded to their attempts with sometimes brutal force. The government banned, arrested, and briefly imprisoned Mandela for his nonviolent attempts at justice. By the 1960s government actions forced Mandela to live underground. He wore disguises, hid away from his family, and worked secretively to organize protests. Finally, in 1961 Mandela and other ANC leaders decided that nonviolence was not going to achieve their freedom: "It was only when all else had failed, when all channels of peaceful protest had been barred to us, that the decision was made to embark on violent forms of political struggle . . . the Government had left us no other choice."

Shortly after the ANC began their armed struggle for freedom, the government captured Mandela and sentenced him to life in prison. He started his prison years in the notorious Robben Island Prison, a maximum-security facility on a small island near Cape Town. In April 1984 the government transferred Mandela to Pollsmoor Prison in Cape Town, and then in December 1988 he was moved again to the Victor Verster Prison near Paarl, from which he was eventually released on February 11, 1990.

The entrance to Robben Island, South Africa—where Nelson Mandela was held captive. The prison, now a museum, is off the coastal city of Cape Town.

In his autobiography, Mandela recalled entering his cell on Robben Island:

> *When I lay down, I could feel the wall with my feet and my head grazed the concrete at the other side. The width was about six feet. . . . I was forty-six years old, a political prisoner with a life sentence, and that small cramped space was to be my home for I knew not how long.*

An Emotional Return

Nelson Mandela revisits his Robben Island cell years later.

Although Robben Island was the harshest facility in the South African prison system, Mandela said, "I never thought that a life sentence truly meant life and that I would die behind bars. . . . I always knew that someday I would once again feel the grass underneath my feet and walk in the sunshine as a free man." There were moments that tried the great man's soul: receiving news of his son's death in an auto crash and his wife's imprisonment for her role in the freedom struggle.

Finally, after almost three decades, world condemnation forced the South African government to free Mandela. Four years later, Mandela became the first president elected after *all* the citizens of South Africa had voted, black and white, in a new nation freed from the oppression of apartheid. As he'd promised, he stepped down after his single term expired in 1999. He spent his remaining years traveling extensively and giving speeches about peace and equality, which he also pursued by establishing both the Nelson Mandela Children's Fund and the Nelson Mandela Foundation. He died at age 95 in 2013, and his funeral was attended by major heads of state from around the world, including the first African American president of the United States, Barack Obama. Obama spoke at the memorial service, saying,

It is hard to eulogize any man—to capture in words not just the facts and the dates that make a life, but the essential truth of a person—their private joys and sorrows; the quiet moments and unique qualities that illuminate someone's soul. How much harder to do so for a giant of history, who moved a nation toward justice, and in the process moved billions around the world.

Besides being president of South Africa from 1994 to 1999, Nelson Mandela spent much of his time as an activist and participating in philanthropies. He founded the Nelson Mandela Legacy Trust, a combination of three charities: the Nelson Mandela Children's Fund, the Mandela Rhodes Foundation, and the Nelson Mandela Centre of Memory.

From the Page to Political Sage: Vaclav Havel

Famous playwright, internationally published author, leader of a movement to free his country from communism, last president of Czechoslovakia, and first president of the Czech Republic: Vaclav Havel led an amazing life. Yet it was not without suffering; for over five years, he was a political prisoner.

Suspicious of his family background, the Communist Party denied Havel the opportunities of a college education, so he took a correspondence course in drama instead. As a young man, he wrote a number of successful plays and worked for the anticommunist magazine *Tvar.*

State authorities imprisoned Havel briefly in 1977 and longer in 1979. In prison he feared for his life under the custody of a man he describes as a "much-feared, half-demented warden." The warden once sighed and told Havel, "Hitler did things differently—he gassed vermin like you right away!" Havel knew imprisonment would be bearable only if he could "breathe some positive significance into it," so he poured himself into his letters to his wife. These letters later became a popular book, *Letters to Olga,* which has been published in a number of languages.

Authorities offered Havel the chance to leave prison if he would also leave the country, but he refused to do so because he was committed to democracy for the Czech people. In late 1983 Havel developed a life-threatening illness. This, coupled with pressure from foreign supporters on the Czech government, led the authorities to release him. After serving time as a political prisoner, Havel had earned a deserved reputation for his commitment to freedom, a factor that led to his later outstanding political career. In 1989 Havel led the Civic Forum party in the "Velvet Revolution" that ousted communism in Czechoslovakia. When democracy was instituted, Havel served two terms as president. After leaving office, he primarily spoke out for environmental issues. He died in 2011 at age 75.

While focusing on environmental issues, Vaclav Havel also became a member of the European Council on Tolerance and Reconciliation.

Text-Dependent Questions

1. What incident made Mohandas Gandhi take an interest in racial equality?

2. Why did Nelson Mandela and his organization have to resort to violence?

3. How long did it take South African leaders to bow to international pressure and release Mandela?

4. How did Vaclav Havel train himself to be a writer when denied a formal education?

Research Projects

1. Research how a recent boycott has led to real political change.

2. Find other writers like Vaclav Havel who became political activists and then politicians.

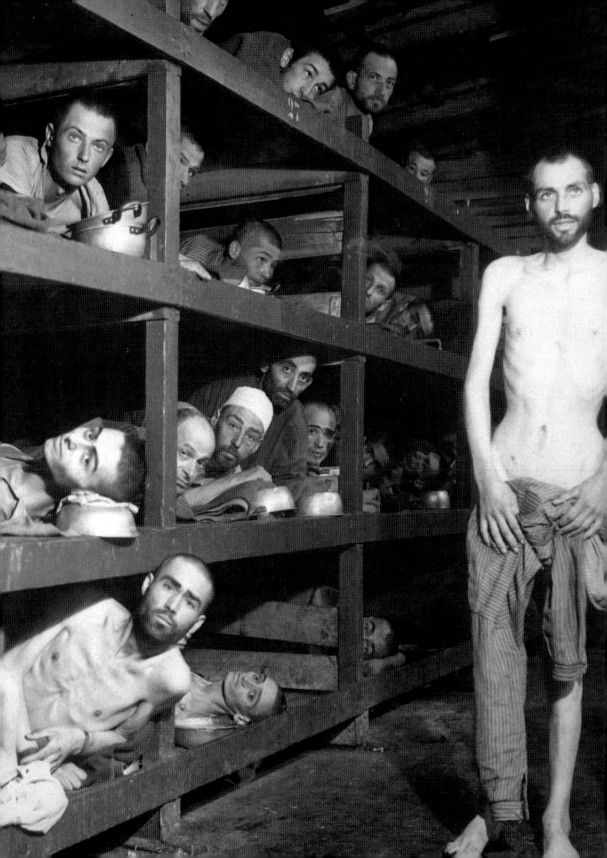

3 Political Prisoners Under Fascism and Communism

Words to Understand

Exile: A punishment that forces a person to leave his or her country; also known as **banishment**.

KGB: The secret police of the former Soviet Union.

Sharashia: A Russian slang term for the prison-based research facility where scientists and intellectuals were forced to work for the government.

Totalitarian: Relating to or operating a centralized government system in which a single party rules over political, economic, social, and cultural life without opposition.

Witch hunt: An intensive effort to expose those considered disloyal or dishonest by the majority, usually based on accusations. It refers to the historical persecution of people labeled as witches.

There may be times when we are powerless to prevent injustice, but there must never be a time when we fail to protest.
— HOLOCAUST SURVIVOR AND AUTHOR ELIE WIESEL

Prisoners at the Buchenwald concentration camp near Weimar, Germany, in 1945. Holocaust survivor Elie Wiesel is in the second row from the bottom, seventh from the left, next to the bunk post.

Making Sure the World Never Forgets: Elie Wiesel

Elie Wiesel, in his famous book *Night,* recounted life in a Holocaust death camp:

> *Never shall I forget that night, the first night in camp, which has turned my life into one long night. . . . Never shall I forget that smoke. Never shall I forget the little faces of the children, whose bodies I saw turned into wreaths of smoke beneath a silent blue sky. Never shall I forget those flames which consumed my faith forever.*

In the 20th century, there were three powerful **totalitarian** governments: the National Socialist (Nazi) government that ruled Germany from 1933 to 1945, the communist government of the Soviet Union that ruled Russia and surrounding nations from 1917 to 1991, and the communist government that has ruled China since 1949. Each of these governments relied on imprisonment as a primary means of political control, and each committed crimes against their own citizens on a massive scale.

Elie Wiesel was born in Sighet, Transylvania, in Romania, on September 30, 1928. He enjoyed his childhood in his Jewish neighborhood that was rich in faith, in community activities, and in loving families. All that changed, however, in 1944, when the Nazis rounded up his family and the rest of the Jewish community and deported them to concentration camps. The Nazis took Wiesel and his father to Auschwitz, separating them from Wiesel's mother and younger sister, Tzipora. Wiesel was 15 at the time, and he never saw his mother or younger sister again. At Auschwitz Wiesel, like all of the other prisoners, was tattooed with an identification number. His was A-7713, a permanent reminder throughout his life of the cruelty and inhumanity he witnessed in that death camp.

An Advocate for the World

Although Wiesel was famous for his brilliant writing about the horrors of those years, his experience was far from unique: more than six million of his fellow Jews died in the Nazi death camps.

After the war, Wiesel vowed never to write about his Holocaust experiences, but in 1955, after meeting the French Catholic novelist and Nobel laureate François Mauriac, he decided to write *Night.* After that first book, he dedicated himself to making sure that the world would never forget what the Nazis did to the Jewish people and others, so that such evil would not happen again. He published more than 50 books; earned the Nobel Peace Prize in 1986 for his message of "peace, atonement and human dignity"; was appointed to chair the President's Commission on the Holocaust; and was awarded the Congressional Gold Medal of Achievement. Wiesel's experiences made him a champion for political prisoners around the world. He traveled to the Soviet Union in 1965 and described the situation of Jews there in his book *The Jews of Silence.* In the years that followed, he worked to bring awareness of political prisoners in the Soviet Union, South Africa, Vietnam, Bangladesh, and elsewhere. Wiesel died in 2016 at the age of 87.

Elie Wiesel speaking alongside President Barack Obama, German Chancellor Angela Merkel, and International Buchenwald Committee President Bertrand Herz.

Fighting Stalin: Alexander Solzhenitsyn

Literary critics regard Alexander Solzhenitsyn as one of the great writers of the 20th century; the rest of the world honors him as an eloquent representative for human rights. His life, with its hardships and punishments, represented the lives of thousands of Russian citizens during the same years. He was born in 1918, six months after his father died fighting for Russia in World War I; his mother, who made her living as a typist, raised him. As a teen, Solzhenitsyn hoped to become a writer, but poverty forced him to go to a local college and study mathematics instead. Later, Solzhenitsyn reflected:

> *I would probably not have survived the eight years in camps if I had not, as a mathematician, been transferred to a so-called **sharashia**, where I spent four years. . . . If I had had a literary education it is quite likely that I should not have survived these ordeals.*

Solzhenitsyn served in the Soviet Army during World War II, fighting on the front line until his own government arrested him in February 1945. He later described

the reason for this arrest: "I was arrested on the grounds of what the censorship had found during the years 1944–45 in my correspondence with a school friend, mainly because of certain disrespectful remarks about Stalin."

A Famous Author Yet Lacking Freedom

During his years of imprisonment and **exile**, Solzhenitsyn had been writing about his experiences, but he did not dare to share his work with the public for fear of losing his life. However, not releasing his work troubled him, and in 1961 he published *One Day in the Life of Ivan Denisovich,* a detailed account of daily life in the Gulag. Communist authorities immediately banned the book, but copies were smuggled to the free world, and Solzhenitsyn the writer became famous in the West. As a result, Solzhenitsyn was awarded the Nobel Prize for Literature in 1970, but he was unable to claim the prize in person due to government travel restrictions.

He spent the next eight years in what the Soviet authorities called "Special Camps." The rest of the world called them the Gulag, and despite the government's nice-sounding name, more than a million political prisoners died from brutal treatment in these incarceration centers.

KGB officers arrested Solzhenitsyn again in 1974 and brought him to Lefortovo Prison. They stripped him, questioned him, and charged him with treason. The next day the Soviet government deprived Solzhenitsyn of his citizenship and deported him to West Germany. From 1975 to 1995 he chose to live in Vermont; he returned to his homeland in 1995.

Despite all the ways he suffered under communism, Solzhenitsyn did not believe that any political party was the major cause of evil in the world. He believed that every person is partially good and partially evil, and therefore each person must undertake to conquer the evil in his or her own heart. His sufferings as a political prisoner and his ability to turn those into powerful writing made Solzhenitsyn one of the greatest writers and thinkers of his time.

Speaking Freely

Alexander Solzhenitsyn delivers a commencement address at Harvard.

Alexander Solzhenitsyn— novelist, historian, and Nobel Prize winner.

Life in the Laogai: Harry Wu

For 19 years, Harry Wu was a political prisoner in China's *laogai,* a vast system of deprivation and punishment. Wu survived against incredible odds, then found his way to the United States. Once in America, he did something even more incredible: Wu risked his life and freedom by returning to China in order to do undercover work documenting the continuing mistreatment of prisoners there.

Wu was raised in Shanghai and influenced by his strict father and kindly stepmother. As a young man, he learned his father's Buddhist customs and the teachings of Italian priests at St. Francis School. These religious teachings later proved to be important. He said, "The sense that human beings are connected to a God, that we should treat one another as God's children, helped sustain me in the dreadful years to come."

In 1949 the Communist Party took over China. For the next seven years, Wu tried to be a "good" communist, yet he was unable to keep quiet when he saw injustices. In I960 a party officer walked into the college classroom where Wu was studying and arrested him. He would spend the next 19 years as a prisoner.

Wu spent almost two decades in the *laogai,* a word that means "reform through labor." In his autobiography Wu wrote,

> Laogai—*the phrase burns my soul, makes me crazy, makes me want to grab Americans and Europeans and Australians and Japanese by the shirt and scream, "Don't you know what's going on over there?" I want the word* laogai *to be known all over the world in the same way that gulag has become synonymous with the horrors of Stalin's prison system.*

The laogai are prisons doubling as factories, where prisoners "have been virtually reduced to slaves." According to Wu's Laogai Research Foundation (www.laogai. org), there are four million to six million Chinese citizens held in these forced-labor camps. The foundation also claims that, since the inception of the laogai, 40 million to 50 million people have been imprisoned: "Almost everyone in China is related to someone or has known someone who has been forced to serve a lengthy sentence in the confines of the Laogai."

In the prison system, Wu battled for his life. As soon as he entered a camp, the guards showed him the bodies of prisoners hung up on meat hooks—the punishment for those who disobeyed their captors. Wu learned to eat captured rats and snakes so he didn't starve. When a friend of Wu's was nearly dead from starvation, he persuaded a guard to bring his friend extra rations. Unfortunately, the extra food was too much for Wu's *starving* friend to digest, and he died "from the surprise of real food." Enraged, Wu cried out in anger at God. Someone—he says it may have been the voice of God or of his father—replied, "Survive. Get through this. Some day you will tell the world."

Wu was beaten by guards, starved, and humiliated, yet survive he did. In 1979 changes in the communist system led the government to release many victims of

the laogai. Wu recalled, "I was forty-two years old. For the first time in my life, I was a free man." However, life in the communist state outside of prison camp was only relatively free. Wu knew party informants were always watching, making sure he did not step out of line with the government; he would have to leave his native country to enjoy a truly free life. In 1983 he witnessed a public execution. He reflected, "I was stunned at how organized it was. This government could not feed its people, but it could kill forty-five people in unison for . . . entertainment and education." This furthered Wu's determination to get out of China.

When Wu received an invitation to speak in Berkeley, CA, in 1985 he jumped at the opportunity to leave China, and at the time, he had no intention of ever returning and sought permanent political asylum in the United States. Life in the United States was not easy at first. He had to sleep in a park some nights, and he worked making donuts, even though he was a highly educated professional in China.

In 1986 Wu had an opportunity to speak about his experiences as a prisoner of conscience in China. He was shocked to learn that Americans did not know anything about the Chinese prison system, and in some cases, they disbelieved him. Although he had just married and was beginning to experience a comfortable life in the United States, Harry Wu decided he would have to take some big risks in order to provide the West with evidence of the cruel treatment endured by millions of his fellow Chinese.

Between 1991 and 1995, Wu returned to China four times, secretly filming and

On April 12, 2000, Harry Wu joined Teamster union members in a march on the U.S. Capitol grounds protesting normal trade relations with China.

documenting conditions of political prisoners in the laogai. In 1991 he posed as a prison guard and carried a hidden camera to produce evidence for the CBS news program *60 Minutes,* documenting that Chinese prisoners were used as slave laborers producing products for export to the West. In 1994 he posed as a wealthy American seeking an organ donor for a sick uncle. He visited 27 labor camps, proving that China was killing prisoners in order to provide organs for wealthy recipients.

In 1995 the Chinese Communist Party arrested Wu, who was then an American citizen, for spying in China. For 66 days, letters and statements of protest came to China from all around the globe. The U.S. Congress passed resolutions condemning the arrest and urging President Bill Clinton to work for Wu's freedom. Due to worldwide concern, the Chinese government gave Wu a mock trial, then expelled him from the country. Back in the United States, Harry Wu continued to seek democracy and freedom for his homeland. After establishing the Laogai Research Foundation, world governments finally began paying attention to the human rights violations in China. Wu also wrote many books on the laogai system and founded the Laogai Museum in Washington, DC. He died at age 79 in 2016.

Leaving the Party: Wei Jingsheng

Dear Deng Xiaoping:

I've written to you so many times now that I'm probably beginning to get on nerves and you're wondering, "Why can't this guy just sit in prison quietly?" This appears to be a real problem, but it is not entirely my fault. I am very capable of staying quiet, but if people don't allow me to be, then I can also be very unquiet. My endless letters and constant badgering are in the tradition of "oppressive government drives the people to rebel."

—A LETTER FROM PRISON FROM WEI JINGSHENG TO
CHINA'S LEADER, NOVEMBER 3, 1989

Wei Jingsheng was born in 1950, one year after the beginning of Communist Party rule in China. His parents were proud longtime members of the party, and they raised him as a member of its "inner circle," thereby allowing him to receive an education in China's most prestigious schools.

In 1966 the "Cultural Revolution" took place, a time when innumerable Chinese citizens were humiliated, imprisoned, or executed over trifling offenses against the Communist Party. The revolution began when Mao Tse-tung—or Chairman Mao as he was called—decided to remove less radical elements of the party. Young zealous party members formed units of the "Red Guard" to purge "Old Guard" elements from the country. The Red Guard forced educated and wealthy members of society to leave their jobs and schools in order to live in poverty in the countryside and "learn from the peasants." Eventually, the Cultural Revolution spun out of control. It became a national **witch hunt** as countless people were accused of disloyalty to the new order. As time went on, the situation spun even more out of control, becoming a civil war, with units of the Red Guard battling each other for control. Wei Jingsheng traveled through the country during this turbulent time, and he witnessed firsthand how the Chinese people suffered under communism; this was the beginning of his loss of faith in the government. He became involved with a magazine protesting the lack of freedom in China.

In 1979 the communist leadership charged Wei Jingsheng with "counterrevolution propaganda and agitation." He spoke in his own defense at the trial, and friends copied down his words, which foreign presses translated and released outside China. The government kept Wei on death row for eight months, then in solitary confinement for the next five years. The Chinese government incarcerated him in two more forced labor camps, where guards treated him very harshly. He suffered from several serious illnesses, which authorities did not treat properly. In 1993 the government released Wei Jingsheng, but six months later, they arrested and tried him again. Authorities convicted Wei of "counterrevolution" and sentenced him to serve another 14 years in the laogai system.

After a total of 18 years in prison, in 1997 the Chinese government authorities took Wei Jingsheng from his prison cell and put him on a plane to the United States, the result of a deal between President Clinton and Chinese president Jiang Zemin. Since 1993 Wei Jingsheng has been nominated seven times for the Nobel Peace Prize. He continues to work tirelessly to promote democratization and the improvement of human rights in China.

Wei Jingsheng during his first press briefing in the United States at the New York Public Library.

Text-Dependent Questions

1. Along with Nazi Germany and the Soviet Union, what was the third major totalitarian world government of the 20th century?
2. What has been the singular focus of author Elie Wiesel's career?
3. Why was Alexander Solzhenitsyn initially arrested in 1945?
4. What is the system of forced factory labor in Chinese prisons called?

Research Projects

1. Research the unique ways other countries imprison and punish their political prisoners.
2. Read other books or accounts by authors about their time as political prisoners. Compare them to the experience of Alexander Solzhenitsyn in the Gulag.

4 Prominent Political Prisoners of the 21st Century

Words to Understand

Atrocities: Shockingly cruel acts of violence against an enemy, particularly in wartime.

Dissidents: Those who publicly disagree with an established political or religious system or organization.

Stand down: To suspend an alert status.

Burma's Heroic Prisoner for Freedom: Aung San Suu Kyi

My Home . . .

where I was born and raised

used to be warm and lovely

now filled with darkness and horror.

My family . . .

whom I had grown with

Former Burmese political prisoner Aung San Suu Kyi receiving the Sakharov Prize for Freedom of Thought in 2013.

used to be cheerful and lively

now living with fear and terror.

My friends . . .

whom I shared my life with

used to be pure and merry

now living with wounded heart.

A free bird . . .

which is just freed

used to be caged

now flying with an olive branch

for the place it loves.

A free bird towards a Free Burma

—AUNG SAN SUU KYI (FROM HER WEBSITE)

On June 19, 2005, Aung San Suu Kyi (pronounced Awn Sawn Sue Chee) received greetings from politicians and celebrities around the world. "I send my best wishes to Aung San Suu Kyi for her 60th birthday," said U.S. president George W. Bush, and his sentiments were echoed by UN Secretary General Kofi Annan, fellow Nobel prize winner South African Bishop Desmond Tutu, exiled Buddhist leader the Dalai Lama, and Czech president and former political prisoner Vaclav Havel. Rock stars joined political and religious leaders in their birthday wishes. In a Dublin concert, rock band REM broadcast a live tribute to her. Lead singer Michael Stipe said, "We want to wish you a happy 60th birthday filled with hope and say that we deeply respect your profound commitment to the people of Burma. . . . And we pray with our hearts that by your 61st birthday, you will walk free among your people." Likewise, Irish rock band U2 sang "Happy Birthday" to the Burmese hero during a sold-out concert, before launching into their song "Walk On," which they had composed years before in her honor.

What did Aung San Suu Kyi think of all these tributes, or did she even know of them? No one can say, for she spent her birthday, as she spent many days before, under strict house arrest. While imprisoned in her own home, she could not leave her dwelling, the government had disconnected her telephone, and her only human contact was with a doctor she saw monthly. Although she is famous internationally, has won the Nobel Peace Prize, and was voted by more than 80 percent of her fellow Burmese citizens to serve as their leader, Aung San Suu Kyi was held as a political prisoner until December 2010. To understand her story, we must learn something about the country of Burma (also called Myanmar), and her father, Aung San.

A Country with Disputed Names

The name of the country was once Burma, but in 1989 the army, which ruled the country, officially changed its name to Myanmar. Opponents of the military government, both within and outside the country, argue that the government does not have the authority to change the country's name. The United Nations recognizes the name Myanmar, but in several countries, including the United States, the United Kingdom, and Canada, it is still referred to as Burma.

Aung San Suu Kyi says, "Burma is one of those countries which seem to have been favored by nature." Writers and travelers have called Burma "the golden land" and "an eastern paradise." It is covered with lush jungle, bordered by blue sea, and favored with a wealth of minerals, precious gems, and stunning architecture. Until the mid-19th century, Burma was a colony of England, although most Burmese desired to rule their own nation. When World War II began, Japanese troops claimed to "liberate" Burma by chasing out the English, but in fact, the Japanese took over the country and ruled it themselves. Burmese freedom fighters joined forces with their former British rulers and fought against the Japanese. When they drove out the Japanese, Burmese leaders and troops insisted on the right to govern their own nation.

The most important person in the struggle for Burma's freedom from foreign governments was a general named Aung San. He had organized Burmese fighters to resist the Japanese, then worked with the British after the war to ensure Burma's freedom. To this day, the Burmese regard Aung San as the "father of his country." Although he is a legendary figure, Aung San did not live to enjoy the freedom he fought for; in 1947 a political rival assassinated him, just months before Britain granted Burma independence.

When he died, Aung San left behind a two-year-old daughter, Aung San Suu Kyi. Parents in Burma rarely name their children after themselves; however, General Aung San broke with tradition, giving his name to his only daughter. Aung San means "victory": to add softness to his daughter's name, he drew from his mother's name, Suu, and from his wife's name, Kyi. Put together, the name Aung San Suu Kyi means "a bright collection of strange victories." It is an unusual name, and its meaning helped give a sense of unusual destiny to the amazing woman who bears it.

Rising to Challenge

Aung San Suu Kyi lived a privileged childhood and young adulthood. After the assassination of General Aung San, the Burmese government appointed Daw Khin Kyi, the general's widow and Aung San Suu Kyi's mother, to serve as ambassador to India. Aung San Suu Kyi then went to live in Delhi with her mother. In India she became aware of Mohandas Gandhi's life and philosophy, knowledge that would influence her later efforts for freedom through nonviolent means.

In the 1960s, while a repressive military government took control of Burma, Aung San Suu Kyi was studying philosophy, politics, and economics at Oxford College in England. At Oxford fellow students noted both her beauty and her strong morals: she wore traditional Burmese clothes such as the sarong and once told fellow students that she would never sleep with anyone except her husband, preferring to "just go to bed hugging my pillow."

While a student in England, she met a fellow scholar named Michael Aris, who was studying Eastern culture and Buddhism; he fell in love with her, but she resisted. Although Aung San Suu Kyi graduated and moved to New York to work for the United Nations and Aris took a job working for the royal family of Bhutan, they kept up correspondence. She was falling in love with the handsome British man, but Aung San Suu Kyi repeatedly wrote him saying that if they were to marry, her commitment to her own Burmese people might have to come before their marriage. "I only ask one thing," she wrote in one letter, "that should my people need me, you would help me to do my duty by them." He agreed, and in 1972 they both returned to England and married. Soon after, they had two children.

For more than a decade, Aung San Suu Kyi and Michael Aris, along with their children, lived happily together. Then Suu Kyi received a phone call: her mother was desperately ill in Rangoon, Burma, and would she come to be by her mother's side? She put down the receiver and began to pack. "I had a premonition," Michael later said, "that our lives would change forever."

Revolution in Waiting

Back in Burma, Aung San Suu Kyi found her homeland in the middle of a revolution. Thousands of students had begun a movement for democracy, which soon gained broad support. As she was already famous as the daughter of the "father of the country," leaders of the revolutionary movement asked her to speak out in favor of democracy. On July 23 the dictatorial ruler of the country, General Ne Win, announced that he was resigning; Aung San Suu Kyi and her fellow citizens were elated, assuming that the people of Burma actually had a chance to take control of their destiny.

On August 8, 1988—known as the "Four Eights," or 8/8/88—student leaders called for a nationwide strike for democracy, and crowds of students, government workers, and Buddhist monks poured into the streets. In response to this protest, President Sein Lwin ordered troops to fire on the demonstrators. Inflamed by this outrage, Aung San Suu Kyi wrote an open letter to the government, proposing democratic elections, then prepared for a major public speech.

On August 26 a sea of people filled an open field beneath the Shwedagon Pagoda, the spiritual and architectural heart of Burma, near the burial site of Aung San Suu Kyi's exalted father, Aung San. There, people climbed trees to catch a glimpse of Aung San's daughter. Her companions warned Aung San

Suu Kyi that someone might try to shoot her during the speech, yet she refused to wear a bulletproof vest.

Her speech was electrifying. Despite the **atrocities** committed by government soldiers, Aung San Suu Kyi told the crowd that they must not hate the army, even as they protested military rule. She said that this moment was "the second struggle for national independence," and the crowd of 100,000 men, women, and children shouted their approval.

The following years were a time of great danger, yet great hope in Burma. The government continued its brutal treatment of democratic leaders and activists, yet the majority of people in Burma continued to hope for real elections and democratic change. For almost a year, Aung San Suu Kyi traveled throughout the country, speaking relentlessly against the military government and in favor of reform. In April 1989 Aung San Suu Kyi and a group of democratic activists were headed for the town of Danubyu when a group of soldiers blocked their way, pointing automatic rifles at them. "Keep moving," Aung San Suu Kyi told her group, then spoke calmly to the soldiers: "Let us pass." There were a few tense moments before an officer rushed up and ordered the soldiers to **stand down**. Later that evening, Aung San Suu Kyi told her fellow activists that if the government killed her, they should use that opportunity "to win democracy and freedom for the country."

House Arrest

On July 20, 1989, soldiers surrounded the office of the democratic party and arrested Aung San Suu Kyi. Her 11-year-old son, Kim, was with her at the time; he asked if the soldiers were going to take her away, and she replied yes. That was the beginning of her first six years of house arrest. Her husband, Michael Aris, was in Scotland for his father's funeral. He hurried to Rangoon, but during the entire six years, the government only allowed him to visit with Aung San Suu Kyi twice. He had to live back in Oxford, taking care of the boys and missing his wife, who, he said, was "the warm heart of the Aris household."

For Aung San Suu Kyi, missing her husband and children became part of the pain of her daily life. The government wanted to tell people that the democracy leader was depressed and dispirited; therefore, she was determined to dress well, stay fit, and act positive. She awoke early each morning, meditated for an hour, exercised on a treadmill, kept the house clean, listened to the radio, read books, and sewed. She dressed neatly each day, putting flowers in her hair.

In 1990 Aung San Suu Kyi's party, the National League for Democracy (NLD), won 82 percent of the national election seats. As party chairperson, Aung San Suu Kyi should have been, according to the vote, leader of the nation. However, the army had no actual intention of honoring the election results; they declared the vote invalid and kept Aung San Suu Kyi under house arrest. The following year

she was awarded the Nobel Peace Prize. Because she was still under arrest, her sons accepted the award on her behalf.

In 1995 the military leaders of Burma (by then renamed Myanmar) allowed Aung San Suu Kyi what they declared to be "freedom," though she was under continual surveillance and not allowed to leave Rangoon. She continued to speak out against the government and in favor of an open democracy. In 1999 her husband phoned from England with the news that he had been diagnosed with cancer. The Myanmar government would not allow him to enter the country, and if Aung San Suu Kyi left, the government would never allow her to return. Aung San Suu Kyi faced her most difficult choice: to leave and be with her husband for his hour of greatest need, or to stay and continue the fight for freedom. Drawing from a life of Buddhist belief and practice, she made her decision by means of prayer and contemplation: "My country first."

In a *Washington Post* article, Ellen Nakashima relates a sad episode at the end of Michael Aris's life:

> *Toward the end of his life, when he was in the hospital, she would try to speak with him every evening. Because her phone line was cut, she arranged to await his call at the home of a diplomat. Military intelligence soon figured it out. One evening, Michael and Suu had just said hello when the line went dead. In a rare moment of utter despair, she burst into tears.*

Michael Aris died in 1999. The next year, the government again arrested Aung San Suu Kyi and held her for 19 months.

After her release, Aung San Suu Kyi toured the country with other activists. On May 30, 2003, a day since recalled by Burmese freedom activists as "Black Friday," a mob armed with bamboo spears surrounded their vehicles and began smashing open windows. They grabbed activists, stripped them, and beat them. Her fellow activists begged Aung San Suu Kyi to flee, but she would not. Her driver gunned their car and raced away from the mob. Activists were convinced this mob attack was a government assassination attempt. Although the government leadership denied that allegation, it is curious that soldiers stopped her vehicle as soon as it escaped from the mob, and once again she was placed under house arrest.

Aung San Suu Kyi was finally released in December 2010. She immediately began pursuing an active role in the government, and her party won 43 of 45 available seats in the 2012 by-elections for Myanmar's Assembly of the Union. In 2015 the NLD secured an 86 percent majority. Unable to run for president due to a technicality (her husband and sons were foreign citizens), Aung San Suu Kyi was named State Counsellor, a specially created office similar to that of a prime minister.

The U.S. Campaign for Burma is dedicated to promoting democracy, human rights, justice, and national reconciliation in Burma. They work to give children a healthy start and the opportunity to learn.

Imprisoned for Speaking Her Own Language: Leyla Zana

Turkish officials released Leyla Zana from prison on June 9, 2004, after a decade of incarceration for the crimes of wearing Kurdish colors on her headband in parliament and speaking her native Kurdish language.

Leyla Zana was born in a small Kurdish village in Turkey in 1961. While still a teenager, she was married to a much older man who was an activist for Kurdish

freedom; he introduced his young wife to the struggle for Kurdish liberation. When she was 15, Leyla gave birth to a son, and shortly after she became the first woman in her town awarded a high school diploma. Five years later, shortly before Leyla gave birth to a daughter, the Turkish government arrested her husband and sentenced him to 30 years in jail. Undaunted, Leyla continued her education and her work for Kurdish freedom and women's rights in Turkey.

Kurds: Persecuted Across Many Nations

Kurds are a large and distinct ethnic minority in the Middle East, numbering some 25 million to 30 million people. They inhabit Iran, Iraq, Syria, and Turkey. In Turkey, Kurds make up 20 percent of the national population, but the founder of modern Turkey, Mustafa Kemal, denied the existence of distinct cultural subgroups in Turkey, so the Turkish government treats any expression of Turkish ethnicity harshly. For example, until 1991 the use of the Kurdish language was illegal, and to this day talk of Kurdish nationalism is controversial and highly discouraged.

In 1991 Zana became famous in Turkey when she became the first woman from the minority Kurdish ethnic group elected to the Turkish parliament. During her oath of allegiance to Turkey's parliament, Leyla Zana said:

> *I swear by my honor and my dignity before the great Turkish people to protect the integrity and independence of the State, the indivisible unity of people and homeland, and the unquestionable and unconditional sovereignty of the people. I swear loyalty to the Constitution.* I take this oath for the brotherhood between the Turkish people and the Kurdish people.

She spoke the italicized sentence in her native Kurdish tongue. After her election, Leyla Zana dared to speak Kurdish in the Turkish parliament and wear the Kurdish colors in the ribbons in her headband, actions that caused an uproar throughout the country and led to her imprisonment. Zana and others have formed a new party, called the Democratic Society Movement, dedicated to defending Kurdish culture as a legitimate part of the Turkish nation. The party was banned by the Turkish government in 2009.

In April 2008 Zana was sentenced to two years' imprisonment by Turkish authorities for "spreading terrorist propaganda" for saying in a speech that Kurds answered to Kurdistan leaders from several nations but did not recognize the government of Turkey. Later that year she received an additional 10-year sentence by a Turkish court because nine more of her speeches similarly preached separatism and terrorism. Those sentences were later overthrown, but Zana remains a very vocal advocate for Kurds in Turkey. In 2011 she was re-elected to Parliament.

After her release from prison, Leyla Zana participated in "Peace and Democracy" rallies in southeastern Turkey.

A Voice for Democracy and Religious Freedom: Father Thadeus Nguyen Van Ly

Father Thadeus Nguyen Van Ly is a Vietnamese Catholic priest who was imprisoned for a total of 15 years because of his involvement in the pro-democracy movement in that country and his defense of freedom of expression and religion. Several advocacy groups, including Freedom Now (freedom-now.org) and Amnesty International, protested Father Ly's mistreatment, resulting in a November 2004 resolution by the U.S. Congress that asked the Vietnamese government to release him. Three months later, Vietnamese authorities released Father Ly.

On June 20, 2005, Vietnamese prime minister Phan Van Kai made a historic visit to the United States. On that same day, Father Ly submitted written testimony to the International Relations Committee of the House of Representatives in Washington, DC, documenting his own mistreatment and that of other **dissidents** at the hands of the Vietnamese government.

In 2006 Father Ly was one of the signers of the Manifesto on Freedom and Democracy, a statement by Bloc 8406, a coalition of political groups calling for democratic reforms in Vietnam. As a result, he was arrested again and sentenced to eight years in prison.

Ahead of a state visit by U.S. President Barack Obama, the Vietnamese government released Father Ly in May 2016.

A Child Imprisoned Because of His Role in the Buddhist Faith: The Panchen Lama Gedhun

The imprisonment of the Panchen Lama is so bizarre and tragic it is almost unbelievable. (*Panchen means* "Great Scholar," and *Lama* is a Tibetan religious teacher. Tibetan Buddhists believe that the Panchen Lama is the protector of all the world's living beings.) The story involves a conquered nation, a reincarnated religious leader, and a communist government attempt to control the spiritual beliefs of the Tibetan people.

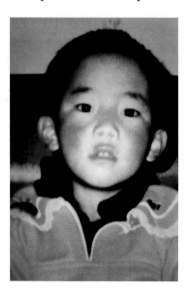

Gedhun Choekyi Nyima was recognized as the 11th Panchen Lama of Tibet by the Dalai Lama. He was abducted by Chinese authorities at age six and has not been seen since.

In 1950 the People's Republic of China announced its intention to "liberate" Tibet, and 40,000 Chinese troops invaded and took control of the little nation. A national uprising nine years later led to the slaughter of 400,000 Tibetans. This led the Chinese authorities to impose their language and education system on the country and to destroy thousands of Buddhist monasteries.

On May 14, 1995, the Dalai Lama, the spiritual leader of Tibet in exile, declared that a six-year-old Tibetan boy, Gedhun Choekyi Nyima, was the reincarnation of the Buddhist leader Panchen Rinpoche, who had died six years earlier. (Reincarnation is the belief that a person's soul after death is reborn in another body.) Three days later, Chinese authorities kidnapped Gedhun and his family, "for his safety." In the two decades since, no one has seen or heard anything of Gedhun or his family. Six months after the kidnapping, the Chinese government forced monks of the Tibetan Buddhist community to meet in Beijing. There, the Chinese presented another young boy they called "the real Panchen Lama." One monk chose suicide rather than accept a religious leader imposed by communist authorities.

Since 2006 the Chinese government's appointed Panchen Lama, Gyancain Norbu, has given many speeches in Tibet, praising the Chinese government for helping the Tibetan people and claiming that Tibetans enjoy full political and religious freedom—statements vigorously denied by Tibetans living in exile. Meanwhile, the Chinese government claims that Gedhun and his family are "free, happy and healthy," living by their own choice at an undisclosed location in China. The government has given no evidence and no specific information to support this claim. In private Tibetan homes and monasteries today there are innumerable portraits of the six-year old-Panchen Lama—not the boy chosen by the Chinese government, but rather the missing child chosen by the Dalai Lama. Buddhists, exiled Tibetans, and numerous supporters around the world continue to request proven information about Gedhun, his location, and his condition.

Text-Dependent Questions

1. Why do some call the Asian nation Burma and others call it Myanmar?
2. What did Aung San Suu Kyi do on "the four Eights"?
3. For what offense was Father Thadeus Nguyen Van Ly persecuted?
4. What became of the Panchen Lama Gedhun Choekyi Nyima?

Research Projects

1. Find a lesser-known individual who was jailed indefinitely for opposing a totalitarian government.
2. Find a lesser-known individual who was incarcerated or persecuted for advocating for religious freedom.

Political Prisoners in the United States?

As the question mark in the chapter title indicates, there is an ongoing debate whether the term political prisoners should apply to certain cases involving the United States. There are differing perspectives on each of these controversial issues.

Victim of Circumstances? Mumia Abu-Jamal

United States Supreme Court Justice Harry Blackmun wrote in 1994, "Even under the most sophisticated death penalty statutes, race continues to play a major role in determining who shall live and who shall die." Legal defender Leonard Weinglass says, "The fight to save Mumia from legal lynching has become the focal point of struggle against the racist death penalty in the U.S." However, the Fraternal Order of Police has stated, "Danny Faulkner was a good and decent man and an honorable police officer. He was brutally murdered, and his killer is Mumia Abu-Jamal."

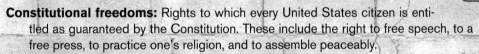

A prisoner of Guantanamo Bay, Cuba, housed in Camp 6 walks in the yard.

Political activist, journalist, and convicted murderer Mumia Abu-Jamal in his prison cell.

Since the shooting of Daniel Faulkner in 1981, the Abu-Jamal case has attracted the attention of many activists and celebrities, as well as organizations from as far away as France and Denmark. Why? Defenders say Abu-Jamal didn't murder Faulkner, but was framed by the Philadelphia police, and will spend the rest of his life incarcerated as a political prisoner.

These are the facts of the case: At 4 a.m. on December 9, 1981, in downtown Philadelphia, police officer Daniel Faulkner stopped a car and arrested its driver, William Cook, for driving down the street in the wrong direction. A short time later, other officers came on the scene and found Faulkner lying dead in the street with bullets in his back and face. Nearby, slumped in a pool of his own blood, lay Cook's brother, Mumia Abu-Jamal, wounded by what was later revealed to be a bullet discharged from Faulkner's gun.

The story gets complicated from there because Abu-Jamal was well known around Philadelphia as a radical black activist. (He had belonged to the Black Panther Party as a teenager.) By 1981 he had become a local radio journalist who sought to expose corruption and mistreatment of minorities in the city. At the time of Faulkner's death, Abu-Jamal was under surveillance by both the FBI and the Philadelphia police.

Abu-Jamal was skeptical if not downright opposed to many government agencies, including the Philadelphia police. In 1968 he attended a protest of **seg-regationist** presidential candidate George Wallace. There, a group of white men attacked him. When a group of white police officers arrived on the scene, they not only let the attack continue, but joined in. In short, there was long-standing animosity between Abu-Jamal and the Philadelphia police.

Waiving his right to a court-appointed lawyer, Abu-Jamal sought to defend himself at his trial for Faulkner's murder, and the judge at first agreed. But after what the judge called some unruly behavior, the judge ordered him to be defended by an attorney. Regardless, the jury found him guilty and sentenced him to death.

After several appeals to Pennsylvania state courts and to the U.S. Supreme Court, as well as after new information surfaced that questioned the evidence, the testimony of witnesses, and the actions of the original judge, Abu-Jamal's conviction was upheld in 2001, but the death sentence was **vacated**. His sentence was changed to life imprisonment without parole. Mumia Abu-Jamal continues to protest his innocence and has written books and essays on social and political issues.

Abu-Jamal's case is emotional in part because it represents a larger issue: the gap between treatment of whites and blacks in the United States justice system. In 2013, for example, 37 percent of state and federal prisoners were black, compared with 32 percent white, 22 percent Latino, and 9 percent other races. Furthermore, blacks are more likely to receive the death penalty. Black men alone make up over 42 percent of all death row prisoners, although they account for only 7 percent of people living in the United States. Although it is a minority view, some critics of the U.S. justice system contend that all blacks incarcerated are political prisoners, since issues of racism and inequality, not connected with individual cases, are a factor in their sentencing.

Hundreds of people have protested the conviction of Mumia Abu-Jamal and call for his freedom. Here, protesters attend a rally at Pershing Square, Los Angeles, at the Democratic National Convention in 2000.

An Ambush Gone Wrong: Leonard Peltier

> *My name is Leonard Peltier.*
> *I am a Lakota and Anishinabe*
> *And I am living in the United States penitentiary,*
> *Which is the swiftest growing*
> *Indian reservation in the country. . . .*
>
> —FROM THE FREE LEONARD PELTIER COMMITTEE WEBSITE

Native American activist Leonard Peltier is still in prison even though he claims he is innocent in the slaying of FBI agents in South Dakota.

Like that of Mumia Abu-Jamal, the case of Leonard Peltier divides observers into two camps. Some see Peltier as a killer, rightfully convicted of killing two law enforcement agents. On the other hand, a large number of supporters around the world, including former attorney general of the United States Ramsey Clark, Nobel Peace Prize winner Bishop Desmond Tutu of South Africa, filmmaker Robert Redford, and numerous Native activists proclaim Peltier's innocence. Peltier says his only guilt is that he was born an American Indian.

In 1975 the Pine Ridge Indian Reservation in South Dakota was experiencing a wave of violence. Activists with the American Indian Movement (AIM) were in conflict with supporters of the tribal council. The tribal council and allegedly the FBI and Bureau of Indian Affairs had armed a group of supporters known as the Guardians of the Oglala Nation (GOONs). Over two years, there were more than 60 murders on the reservation. Many of these deaths remain unsolved. The mid-1970s were a period of terrible pain for the people at Pine Ridge, and many mysteries remain concerning the events of that time. Leonard Peltier's incarceration is one legacy of what some still call "the reign of terror."

All accounts agree that FBI agents Jack Coler and Ronald Williams drove onto the Jumping Bull Compound of the reservation at a time when Leonard Peltier and several companions from AIM were camping there to protect a family. There was a firefight. Peltier claims he and his friends were uncertain who the combatants were, and they later found the two agents dead after the battle. The FBI claims Peltier himself killed the agents. Large numbers of FBI agents and GOONs then moved into the compound. Peltier and his companions escaped, eventually arriving in Canada. Later, Canada sent Peltier back to the United States to face trial. Separate courts tried two of Peltier's AIM friends who were with him that day, and they were found not guilty by reason of self-defense.

Solitary Confinement

A former guard describes Leonard Peltier's time in solitary confinement.

Peltier, however, was tried, convicted of murder, and sentenced to two life sentences. Peltier's supporters claim the trial was unfair. They say that the government's key witness, allegedly Peltier's girlfriend, was someone Peltier had never even met before the trial, and that the murder weapon was never in Peltier's possession. Government supporters in turn dispute all these claims, and say the trial was fair and just. Like Mumia Abu-Jamal, many consider Leonard Peltier a political prisoner since his case involves larger issues of justice.

Guantanamo Bay Military Prison

Guantanamo is a U.S. military base on Cuban soil, which has been operational for over a century. A 1903 agreement with Cuba gave the United States "complete jurisdiction and control" of the Guantanamo Bay base. In recent years, the

The view from the Northeast Gate of Guantanamo Bay looks out at Cuban territory.

REPUBLICA DE CUB
TERRITORIO LIBRE DE AMERIC

NORTH EAST GA
MARINE CORPS SECURITY FORCE CO
U.S. NAVAL BASE
GUANTANAMO BAY, CUBA

U S M C

site has become the subject of international controversy for its prison, which holds mostly suspected terrorists from Afghanistan and other countries. As of October 2016, 60 prisoners remain in the facility. One of those recently released was Mohamedou Ould Slahi, a Mauritanian who was held at Guantanamo for 14 years. While there, he kept a handwritten journal, which was later published as **Guantánamo** Diary.

Gitmo: Prison of Scandal

"Gitmo," as it is commonly called, has become a flashpoint for international controversy regarding the treatment and rights of prisoners. The U.S. government's stated position is that the United States is in a war and therefore must treat terrorist enemies in ways that differ from ordinary imprisonment; this will protect the United States from attack and help get information vital to national security. On the other hand, international groups such as the Red Cross and Amnesty International, as well as some U.S. citizens, including former president Jimmy Carter, believe that violations of international standards at Guantanamo harm American interests and are unworthy of the country's ideals.

Torture at Gitmo?

There have been multiple **allegations** of mistreatment of prisoners at Guantanamo. Three British citizens, released in 2004 without any charges ever filed against them, say they suffered torture, sexual humiliation, and denial of religious freedom at the facility. Moazzam Begg, freed in January 2005, after nearly three years in captivity at Guantanamo, accuses American soldiers of torturing prisoners from Afghanistan and Pakistan, claiming he "witnessed two people get beaten so badly that I believe it caused their deaths." Seven guards were later charged in connection with those deaths. On November 30, 2004, the *New York Times* released excerpts from a report by the International Committee of the Red Cross, stating that conditions at Guantanamo were "tantamount to torture." More recently, the *New York Times* quoted an FBI agent as saying, "On a couple of occasions, I entered interview rooms to find a detainee chained hand and foot in a fetal position to the floor, with no chair, food or water. Most times they had urinated or defecated on themselves and had been left there for 18, 24 hours or more."

The U.S. government disputed all these claims. In June 2005 Vice President Dick Cheney defended conditions at Guantanamo, saying, "They're very well treated down there. They're living in the tropics. They're well fed." When Barack Obama ran for the presidency in 2008, he promised to immediately close the Guantanamo prison. In early 2016 President Obama sent his closure plans to Congress for approval. By that time there were only 80 inmates left in the facility, the smallest population since 2002.

Camp Delta—a recreation and exercise area in Guantanamo.

The unusual legal status of Guantanamo Bay was a factor in the choice of that location as a prison center. The U.S. government claimed that because Gitmo is on Cuban soil, prisoners there do not have the constitutional rights they would otherwise have if they were on U.S. soil. For example, prisoners can be held without charges brought against them, without legal representation by a lawyer, for an indefinite length of time—all of which would be violations of U.S. civil rights. However, the Supreme Court rejected this argument in a 2004 case on the grounds that the United States has exclusive control over Guantanamo Bay. The Cuban government has consistently called the presence of the U.S. base on Cuban soil illegal under international law.

The PATRIOT Act

Following the attacks of September 11, 2001, the U.S. Congress passed the USA PATRIOT Act (Uniting and Strengthening America by Providing Appropriate Tools Required to Intercept and Obstruct Terrorism Act of 2001). This act, which passed with support by both Republicans and Democrats, broadened the abilities of U.S. law enforcement agencies to conduct searches and detain and deport prisoners regarded as potential terrorists. In June 2005 President George W. Bush stated that terrorism investigations under the act had resulted in more than 400 charges, more than half of which resulted in convictions, although in some of these cases, prosecutors chose to charge suspects with non-terror-related crimes such as immigration fraud. Critics of the PATRIOT Act have especially objected to "sneak and peek" searches, in which government agents may search a person's home or business without notifying the subject of the search—an action that would otherwise violate citizens' constitutional rights. A 2005 Amnesty International report criticized the unlawful detainment without charge of several U.S. citizens, another example of civil rights violations conducted under the act.

According to a report released in 2005 by Human Rights Watch (hrw.org) and the American Civil Liberties Union (aclu.org), "Operating behind a wall of secrecy, the U.S. Department of Justice thrust scores of Muslim men living in the United States into . . . indefinite detention without charge and baseless accusations of terrorist links." The report documented that the government detained 69 Muslims shortly after the September 11, 2001, terrorist attacks; the government charged fewer than half of them with a crime and did not inform many of them of the reason for their arrests. Many were not allowed immediate access to a lawyer and were not permitted to see the evidence used against them. According to the report,

> *Witnesses were typically arrested at gunpoint, held around the clock in solitary confinement, and subjected to the harsh and degrading high-security conditions usually reserved for prisoners accused or convicted of the most dangerous crimes. Corrections staff verbally harassed the detainees and, in some cases, physically abused them.*

The U.S. government has not confirmed these allegations. However, seven military prosecutors resigned or asked for reassignment because they were concerned that Guantanamo Bay military trials weren't fair. At least eight prisoners were convicted in this way. And according to the 2016 ACLU report "Guantanamo by the Numbers," nine inmates died in custody, including seven by suicide.

Freedom versus Public Safety: Difficult Issues for the United States

Alleged mistreatment of prisoners at Guantanamo Bay and abuses of persons under the PATRIOT Act are problems related to a difficult moral question: At what point should a government violate some people's rights in order to protect

others from possible attacks? A poll by the Gallup organization found that almost half of U.S. citizens interviewed would be willing to give up some of their **constitutional freedoms** in order to prevent future terrorist attacks.

Trading civil rights for security seems logical to some citizens. Isn't it better to jail or torture a few people than to allow many people to suffer from terrorist attacks? However, historians and philosophers caution against thinking that "the ends justify the means," pointing out that the Nazis and Russian communists, for example, noted for human rights abuses, operated on just such assumptions. Harsh treatment of prisoners and unconstitutional invasions of privacy could make the United States safer, but should a nation that has led the world in freedom resort to the same methods it has criticized in other countries? These are difficult questions, and future citizens will have to carefully discuss and act on them.

Text-Dependent Questions

1. Why is Mumia Abu-Jamal's guilt in question?
2. What are some inconsistencies that cast doubt on Leonard Peltier's conviction?
3. What individuals or organizations have expressed opposition to the treatment of prisoners in Guantanamo Bay?

Research Projects

1. Research Guantanamo Bay Naval Base. How was the prison facility at Guantanamo used before 9/11? Were there any controversies?
2. Research other individuals who have possibly been wrongfully detained for long periods of time under the PATRIOT Act.

6 The Struggle for Freedom Continues

Please use your liberty to promote ours.

—Aung San Suu Kyi

Dr. Wang Bingzhang is serving a life sentence in a prison in Guangdong Province, China, a punishment for political "crimes" related to his involvement in the Chinese **pro-democracy movement**. Born in China, Wang graduated from Beijing Medical University, practiced as a doctor, and earned a PhD in 1982 from McGill University in Montreal, Canada. While overseas, he established a pro-democracy magazine, *China Spring*. He later went back to China and helped organize two **opposition parties** there, the Chinese Freedom Democracy Party and the Chinese Democracy Justice Party. He was arrested and expelled from China for these activities. He worked for decades writing articles and organizing groups on behalf of Chinese democracy, all done as a Chinese citizen in exile.

I've always felt that if I can't get him released, the second best thing would be for him to know that his sacrifice had not been in vain. I feel

Advocacy groups, such as Human Rights Watch and Amnesty International, help to focus world attention on the problem of political prisoners. The candle wrapped in barbed wire is Amnesty International's symbol.

it is my responsibility to keep sharing his story because in a sense I'm privileged to be able to do this.

—TI-ANNA WANG, DAUGHTER OF DR. WANG BINGZHANG

In 2002 Wang and two companions traveled to Vietnam to meet with supporters of democracy in China. While there he was abducted by Chinese secret agents and taken to China. In 2003 he was convicted of **espionage** and terrorism after a secret trial and was sentenced to life imprisonment, despite protests from the United Nations, Amnesty International, and other groups.

Although the Chinese government continues to claim that Wang is a "terrorist," Thai police **exonerated** him in August 2005 of any connection to a plot to bomb the Chinese embassy in Bangkok. This had been the key charge in the Chinese government's case against Wang. According to Wang's family and supporters, physical abuse by guards has increased in recent years, and Wang suffers from poor health. He is one of thousands of men, women, and even a few children imprisoned in various nations today for political reasons.

Ti-Anna Wang (right) holds a photo of her imprisoned father during a U.S. House of Representatives hearing called "Their Daughters Appeal to Beijing: Let Our Fathers Go!" held by the House subcommittee on global human rights

Fighting to Free Her Father

A daughter struggles to free her father held as a political prisoner in China.

Asia

China has certainly changed in recent years, with a new openness to capitalism, trendy styles, and innovative artists and inventors coming to the forefront of Chinese society. However, human rights are still a concern, as the kidnapping of Dr. Wang Bingzhang demonstrates. A recent Amnesty International report notes that the government often labels political dissidents or religious figures "terrorists," then imprisons or executes them. There are even reports of prisoners killed for sale of organs.

Working to Free Political Prisoners

Explaining how an Amnesty International letter-writing campaign improved his situation as a political prisoner, Professor Luiz Rossi of Brazil said, "I knew that my case had become public. . . . Then the pressure on me decreased and conditions improved. Countless men, women, and children around the world today are political prisoners. By working together, staying informed, and using the power of their influence, citizens around the globe can help to bring freedom to political prisoners like Rossi.

Human Rights Watch reported, "In spite of China's rhetoric about legal reform . . . the Chinese government still does not tolerate uncontrolled political or religious activity." This is true in occupied Tibet as well as mainland China.

Burma (Myanmar) also continues to imprison dissidents. As of July 2016 the Burmese government incarcerated nearly 300 political rights activists. In addition, the government has forced some half million ethnic minority members to relocate to government-sponsored centers or projects, and there are numerous recent cases of religious persecution as well.

The Middle East

One major change in the first years of the 21st century was the defeat of Saddam Hussein's Ba'ath Party control over Iraq following U.S. military intervention. Hussein's regime had imprisoned and tortured many political dissidents.

That is not the only example of political imprisonment in the Middle East. For example, in Egypt hundreds of members of the Muslim Brotherhood, a Sunni Islam religious and political group, were killed and hundreds of others arrested and jailed. This followed a crackdown on the group after the 2013 overthrow of President Mohamed Morsi, who was a member of the Brotherhood and the first president elected by the Brotherhood's Freedom and Justice Party. The organization has been declared a terrorist group by the current Egyptian government and banned.

Syria has a history of political imprisonment. From 1964 to 2011, when civil war broke out in the country, government forces were legally allowed to hold political suspects for an unlimited time. Thousands of people were arrested, tortured, and held for months or years without trial. Since the war began, activists, journalists, and humanitarian workers reportedly have been targeted by government forces and pro-government militias. One organization, the Syrian Observatory for Human Rights, claimed in 2015 that about 200,000 Syrians had been arrested by government forces since 2011 and that nearly 13,000 people, including 108 children, had been tortured to death in prisons.

Saudi Arabia also has a history of imprisoning dissidents and political activists. According to a 2015 report by Human Rights Watch, "Saudi authorities continued arbitrary arrests, trials, and convictions of peaceful dissidents. Dozens of human rights defenders and activists continued to serve long prison sentences for criticizing authorities or advocating political and rights reforms."

Africa

In Ethiopia government forces have killed or imprisoned thousands of citizens who oppose the government. The police and the military have conducted mass arrests of protesters, journalists, and opposition party members. In Sudan, as part of the civil war that led to the establishment of South Sudan, military groups allied with the main government killed, raped, enslaved, and relocated masses of civilians. In Ivory Coast, the recent civil war resulted in political killings, massacres, "disappearances," and torture. In Eritrea, a rebel group seized power from the formerly Ethiopian-aligned government, and it rules with an iron fist. Unfriendly political parties have been banned, and according to a 2013 report by Amnesty International, more than 10,000 people who opposed the government in some way are housed in a secretive network of shipping containers and underground cells.

Amnesty International and Other Organizations that Work on Behalf of Political Prisoners

You may think, There are so many political prisoners and so many nations that abuse human rights; what difference can someone like me make in the world? In fact, individuals can make a difference. Former political prisoners say repeatedly that the actions of people around the world made a difference in their situation. Protests, emails, letters, and even prayers from concerned people sustained them and eventually brought about their release.

Several organizations are dedicated to supporting political prisoners. Some organizations, like the International Leonard Peltier Defense Committee (whoisleonardpeltier.info), commit themselves to one person's cause. Others, like the U.S. Campaign for Burma (uscampaignforburma.org), focus on prisoners within one nation. Amnesty International is a large international organization dedicated to protecting human rights all over the world. Begun in 1961, Amnesty International now has seven million members in 160 countries. The top

goals of the organization are freedom for prisoners of conscience, fair and prompt trials for political prisoners, and an end to the death penalty, torture, and other cruel treatment. Amnesty International conducts campaigns and "urgent actions," requesting letters and faxes to be sent on behalf of specific prisoners. Members write the government of the detainees, urging their release and informing them that people around the world are concerned.

Members of Amnesty International take part in a demonstration in Warsaw, Poland.

Text-Dependent Questions

1. How did Dr. Wang Bingzhang, an exiled Chinese citizen who lived primarily in Canada, come to be imprisoned in China?
2. What are some ways to raise awareness of and fight for the release of a political prisoner?
3. What is one of the primary goals of Amnesty International?

Research Projects

1. Research a political prisoner whom you think has been unfairly imprisoned.
2. Research a now-freed political prisoner. Write about what that person did that led to his or her imprisonment.

Series Glossary

Abolition: The act of officially ending a law or practice.

Acquitted: Declared not guilty by a court or judge.

Adjudicated: Made a legal decision.

Advocacy: Active support for a cause or position.

Allegations: Statements saying someone has done something wrong or illegal.

Arbitrary: Based on whim or chance instead of logic.

Arson: The willful and malicious burning of property.

Asylum: Protection given by a government to someone who has left another country to escape being harmed.

At-risk: In danger of being harmed or damaged; in danger of failing or committing a crime.

Chronic: Something that is long term or recurs frequently.

Civil rights: Basic rights that all citizens of a society are supposed to have.

Coerce: Force someone to do something he or she does not want to do.

Community service: Unpaid work performed for the benefit of the local community that an offender is required to do instead of going to prison.

Constitutional freedoms: Rights to which every United states citizen is entitled as guaranteed by the Constitution. these include the right to free speech, to a free press, to practice one's religion, and to assemble peaceably.

Corporal punishment: Punishment that involves inflicting physical pain.

Court-martialed: Tried and convicted in a military court.

Defendant: In a criminal trial, the person accused of a crime.

Disposition: Settlement of a legal matter.

Detainees: People being detained, or kept in prison.

Disposition: Settlement of a legal matter.

Dissidents: Those who publicly disagree with an established political or religious system or organization.

Electronic monitoring: Electronic or telecommunications system, such as an ankle bracelet transmitter, used to track and supervise the location of an individual.

Exile: A punishment that forces a person to leave his or her country; also known as banishment.

Exonerated: Cleared of criminal charges or declared not guilty.

Extenuating circumstances: Reasons that excuse or justify someone's actions.

Extortion: The crime of obtaining something from someone using illegal methods of persuasion.

Extrajudicial: Outside normal legal proceedings.

Felonies: Serious crimes for which the punishment is usually imprisonment for more than a year.

Fraud: The crime of obtaining money or other benefit by the use of deliberate deception.

Grievance: A written complaint, delivered to authorities for resolution.

Halfway house: A residence for individuals after release from institutionalization (for a mental disorder, drug addiction, or criminal activity) that is designed to facilitate their readjustment to private life.

Hearing: Formal discussion of an inmates' case before a judge.

Humane: Having or displaying compassion.

Hunger strike: A refusal to eat, usually carried out by a prisoner as a form of protest.

Indicted: Formally charged someone with a crime.

Industrialized: Adapted to industrial methods of production and manufacturing.

Inherent: Innate or characteristic of something, and therefore unable to be considered separately.

Inhumane: Without compassion; cruel.

Inquest: A formal legal investigation.

Jurisdiction: A territory over which a government or agency has legal authority.

Larceny: The unlawful taking of personal property from another.

Lynching: Seizing someone believed to have committed a crime and putting him or her to death immediately and without trial, often by hanging.

Mandate: An order handed down by a governmental authority.

Misdemeanors: Minor crimes considered less serious than felonies.

Objective: Unbiased by personal feelings or interpretations.

Organized crime: Criminal activities that are widespread and centrally controlled like a business.

Parole: The early release of a prisoner with specified requirements, such as the need to report to authorities for a specified period.

Penology: The study of the treatment of criminals and incarceration.

Peremptory: Not open to debate or discussion.

Plea bargains: The negotiations of agreements between prosecutors and defendants whereby defendants are permitted to plead guilty to reduced charges.

Precedent: An action or decision that can be used as an example for a later decision or to justify a similar action.

Probation: A period where an offender is released from prison but placed under supervision.

Protocols: Detailed rules and plans.

Psychotherapy: The treatment of mental illness through analysis or talk therapy.

Public-order crimes: Victimless crimes, such as prostitution.

Punitive: Inflicting or intended as punishment.

Quarantine: To separate to prevent contact.

Radical: Extreme.

Recidivism: The repeating of or returning to criminal behavior. The recidivism rate is the percentage of released prisoners who go on to commit new crimes.

Rehabilitation: To help someone return to good standing in the community.

Retribution: Punishment.

Repent: To express regret and seek forgiveness for past deeds, such as crimes.

Restitution: The act of making good or giving an equivalent for some injury.

Self-incrimination: The act of offering evidence or statements that would strongly suggest one's own guilt.

Shanks: Makeshift knives made out of other objects.

Sociopaths: People whose behavior is antisocial and who lack a conscience.

Status offender: A young person charged with an offense, such as running away from home or skipping school repeatedly, that would not be considered a crime if com- mitted by an adult.

Suspended sentences: Punishments that are not carried out so long as the person meets certain conditions.

Therapeutic: Helpful toward solving or curing a physical problem or illness.

Tribunal: A court or forum of justice.

Truancy: Being absent from school without an excuse.

Vagrancy: A lifestyle characterized by wandering with no permanent place to live.

Work-release program: A program that allows trusted offenders to work outside the correctional facility.

Workhouses: Publicly supported buildings where usually very poor people worked in exchange for housing and food.

Further Resources

Websites

Amnesty International: *www.amnesty.org*

Daw Aung San Suu Kyi: *www.dassk.org/index.php*

Human Rights Watch: *hrw.org*

U.S. Campaign for Burma: *www.uscampaignforburma.org*

Wei Jingsheng Foundation: *www.weijingshengfoundation.org*

Further Reading

Amnesty International. *Freedom: Stories Celebrating the Universal Declaration of Human Rights*. New York: Broadway Books, 2011.

Aung San Suu Kyi. *Freedom from Fear and Other Writings*. New York: Viking, 1991.

Fischer, Louis. *Gandhi: His Life and Message for the World* (reprint ed.). New York: Signet, 2010.

Havel, Vaclav, and Paul Wilson. *Letters to Olga*. New York: Henry Holt, 1989.

Wei Jingsheng. *The Courage to Stand Alone*. New York: Viking, 1997.

Mandela, Nelson. *Long Walk to Freedom: The Autobiography of Nelson Mandela*. New York: Black Bay Books, 1995.

Oufkir, Malika. *Freedom: The Story of My Second Life*. New York: Miramax Books/Hyperion Press, 2006.

Solzhenitsyn, Alexander. *One Day in the Life of Ivan Denisovich*. New York: Bantam, 1984.

Wiesel, Elie.

Night (rev. ed.). trans. Marion Wiesel. Boston: Hill & Wang, 2006.

Wu, Harry. *Troublemaker: One Man's Crusade Against China's Cruelty*. New York: Random House, 1996.

Zantovsky, Michael. *Havel: A Life*. New York: Grove Press, 2014.

Index

About the Author

Roger Smith holds a degree in English education and formerly taught in the Los Angeles public schools. Smith did volunteer work with youthful inmates at a juvenile detention facility in Los Angeles. He currently lives in Arizona.

About the Series Consultant

Dr. Larry E. Sullivan is Associate Dean and Chief Librarian at the John Jay College of Criminal Justice and Professor of Criminal Justice in the doctoral program at the Graduate School and University Center of the City University of New York. He first became involved in the criminal justice system when he worked at the Maryland Penitentiary in Baltimore in the late 1970s. That experience prompted him to write the book *The Prison Reform Movement: Forlorn Hope* (1990; revised edition 2002). His most recent publication is the book *The Brownsville Boys: Jewish Gangsters of Murder, Inc. (*2013)*. At John Jay College, in addition to directing the largest and best criminal justice library in the world, he teaches graduate and doctoral level courses in criminology and corrections. John Jay is the only liberal arts college with a criminal justice focus in the United States and is internationally recognized as a leader in criminal justice education, research, and training.

Picture Credits